Introducing my enchanting coloring book of mythical creatures!

ASMO

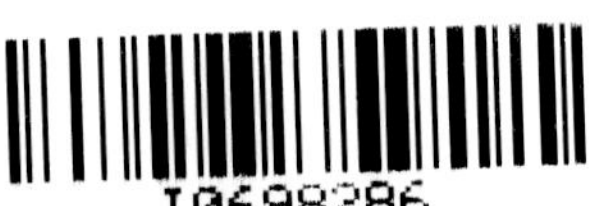

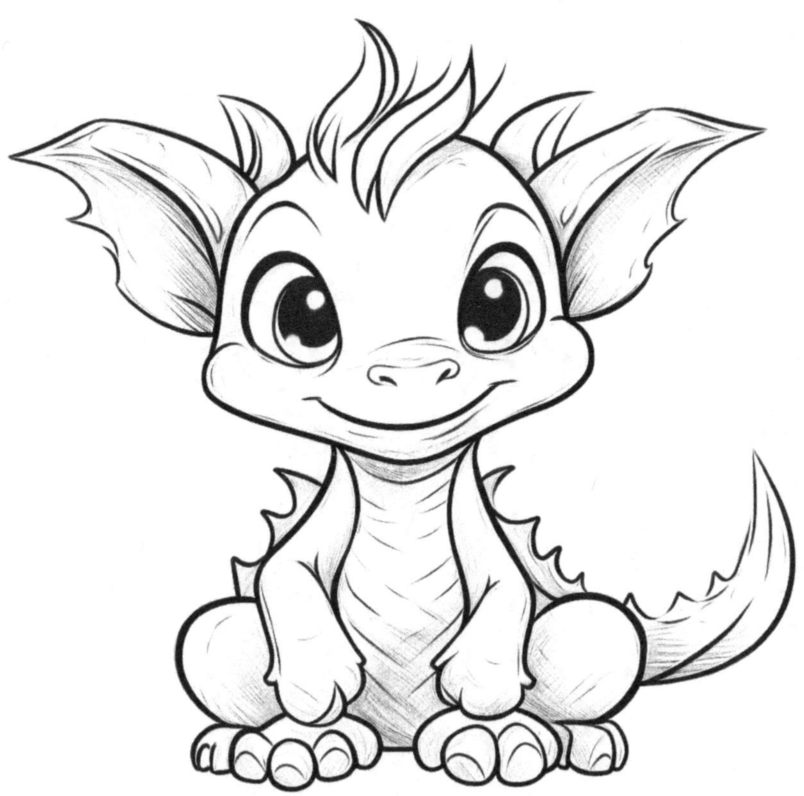

This book belongs to

____

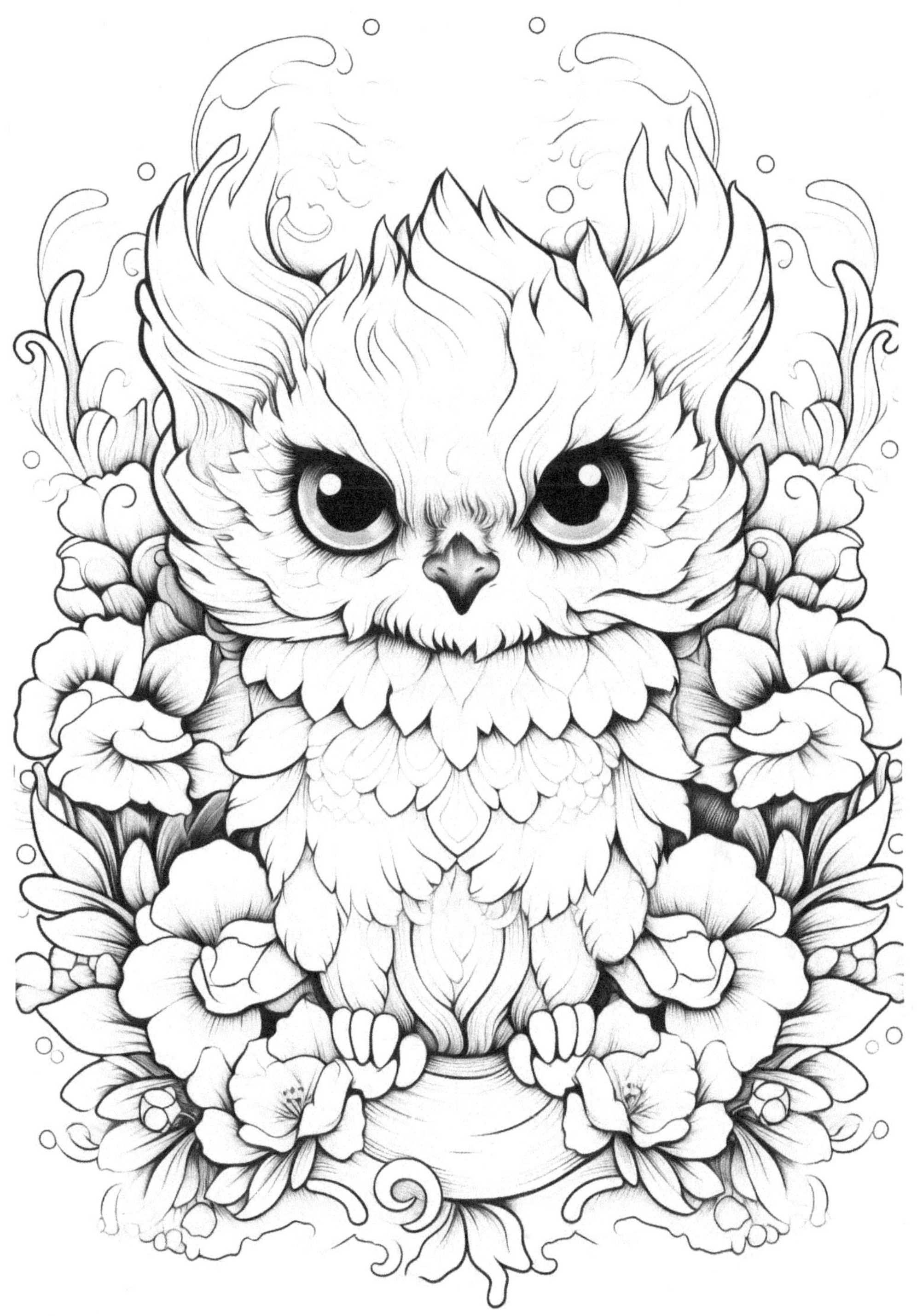

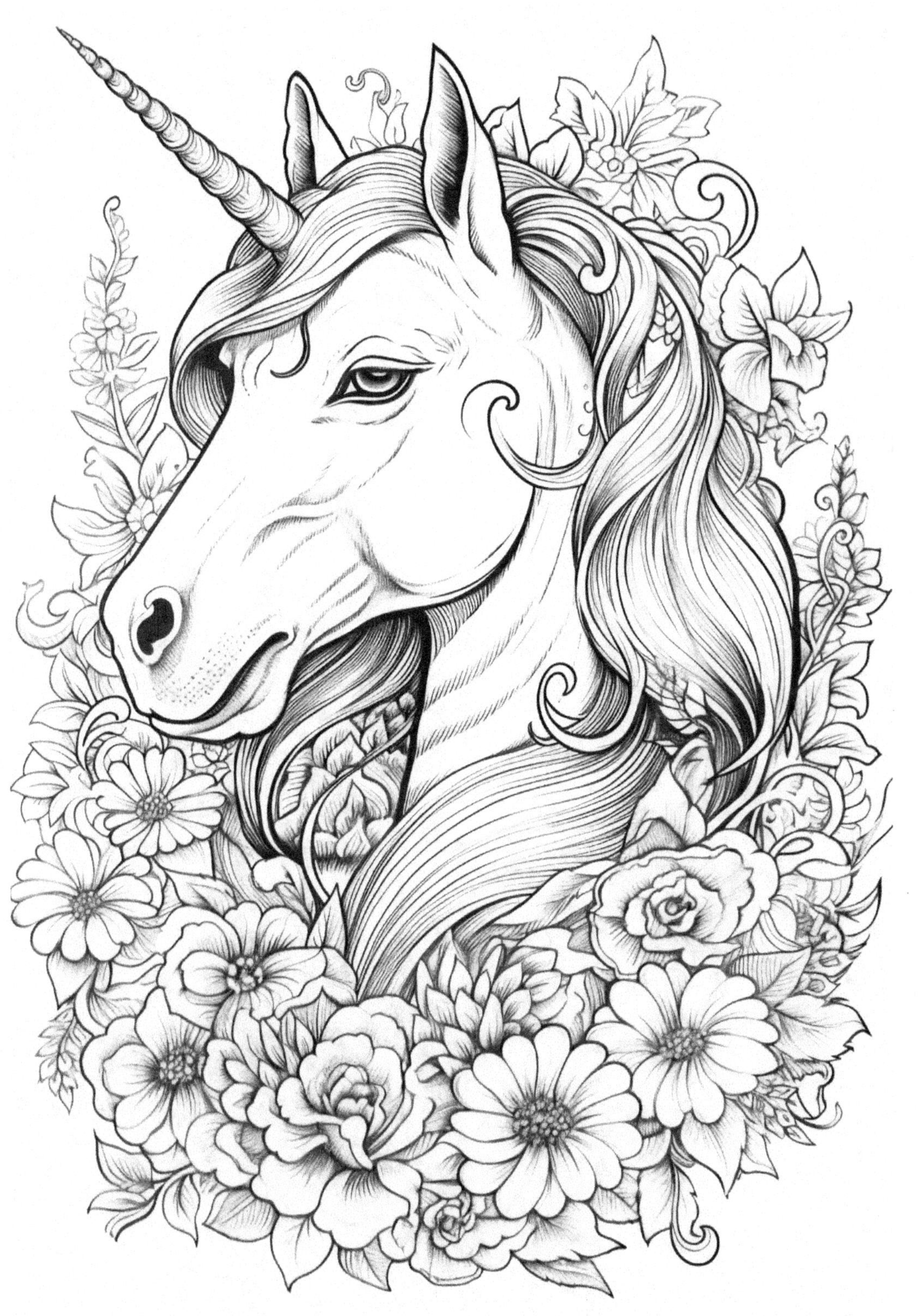

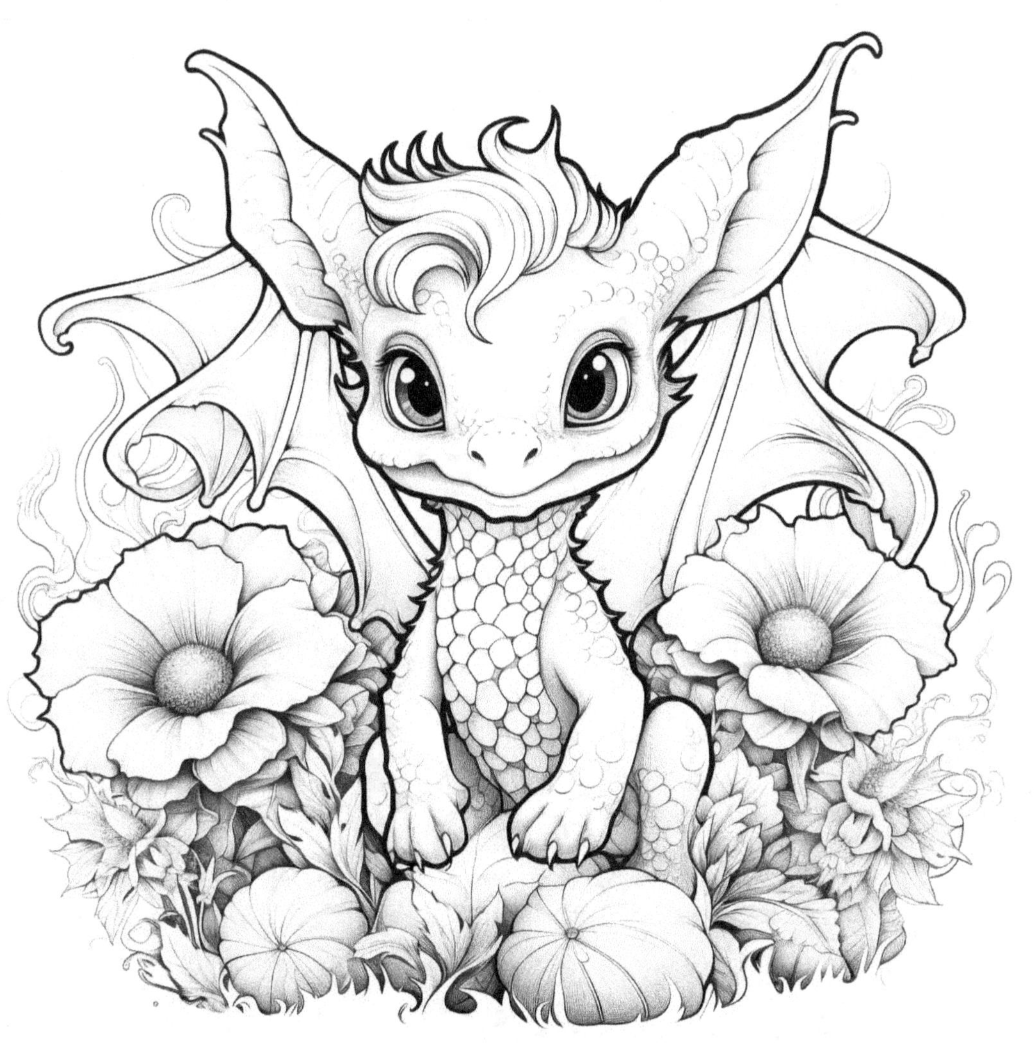

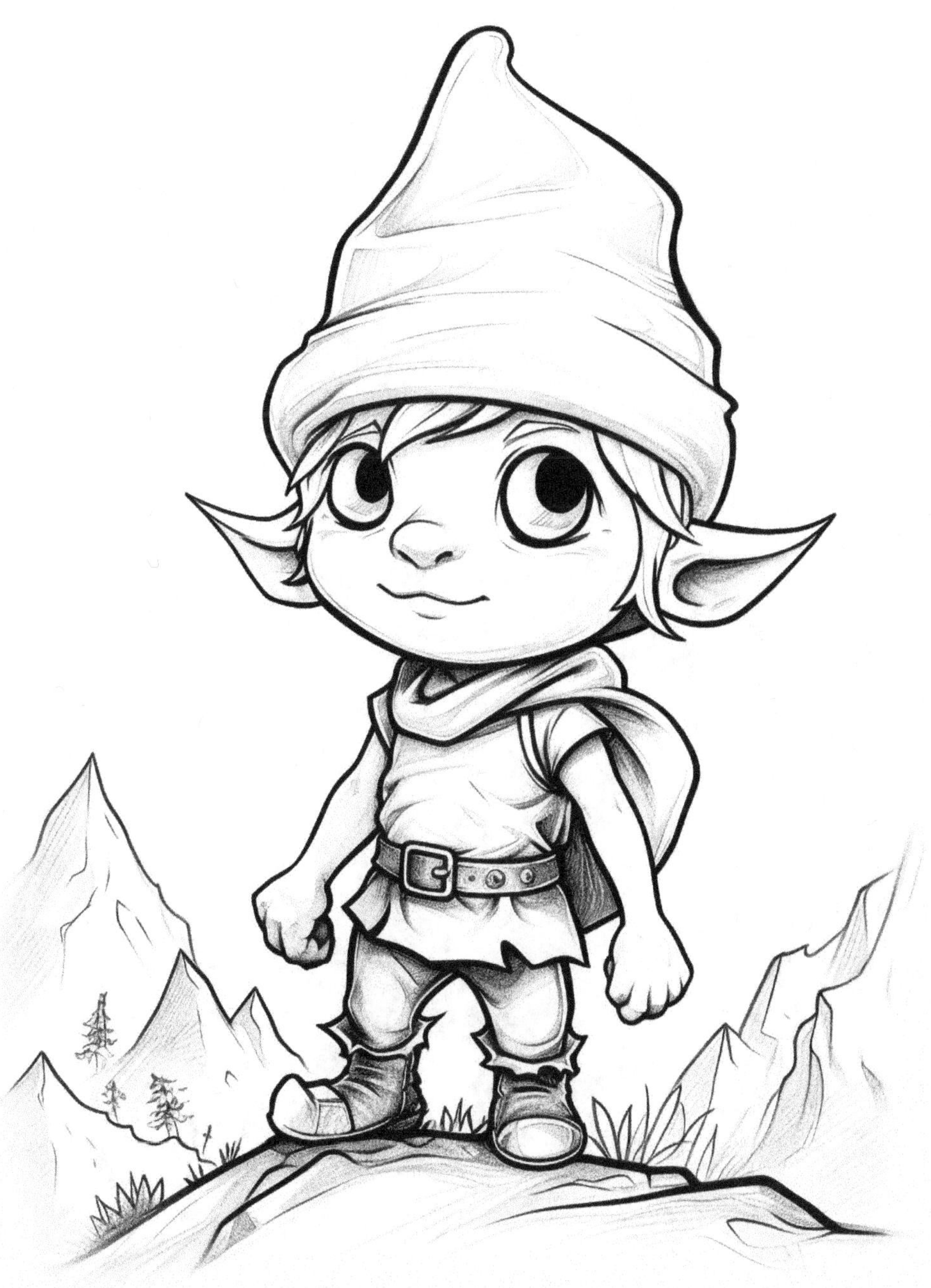

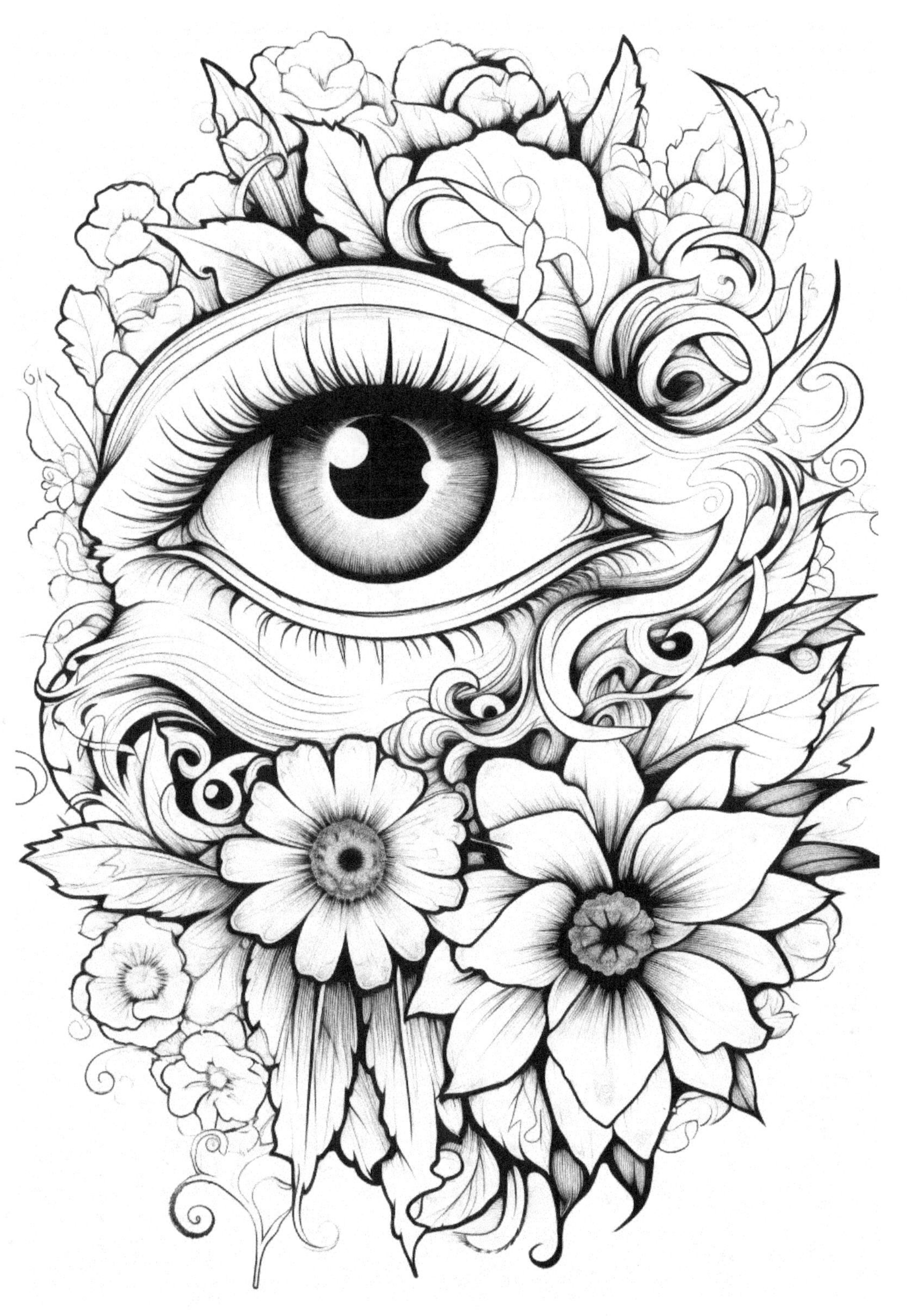

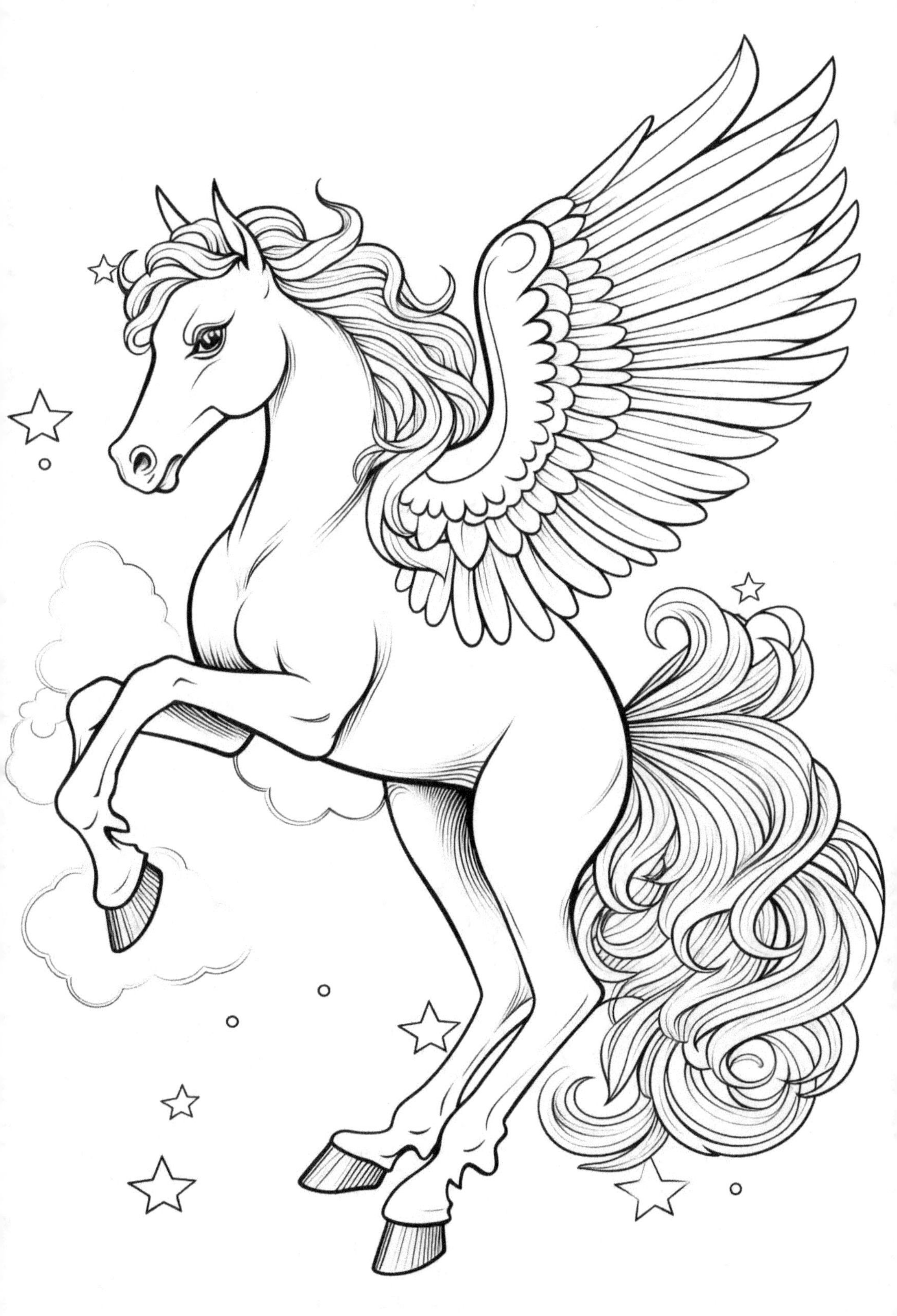

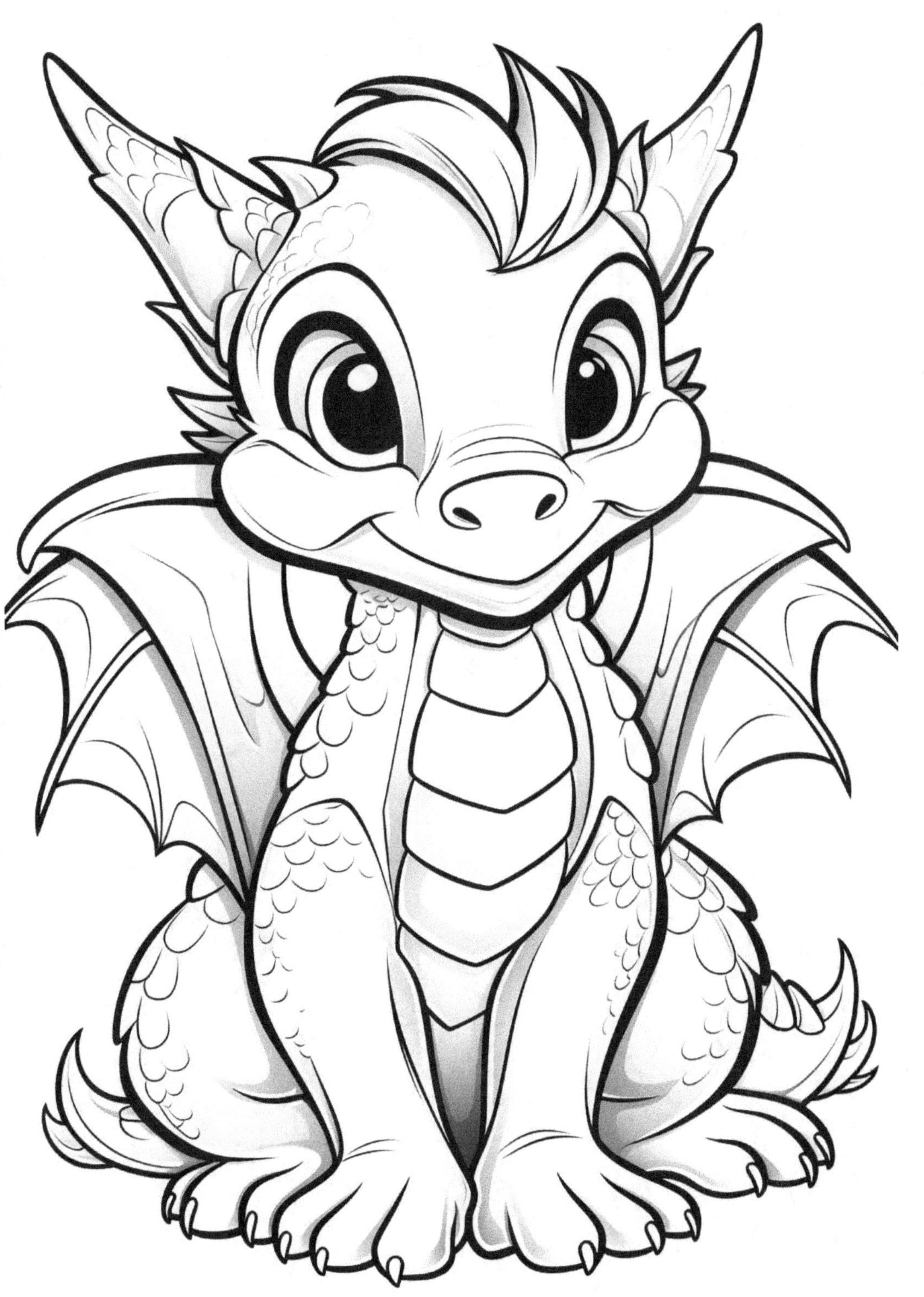

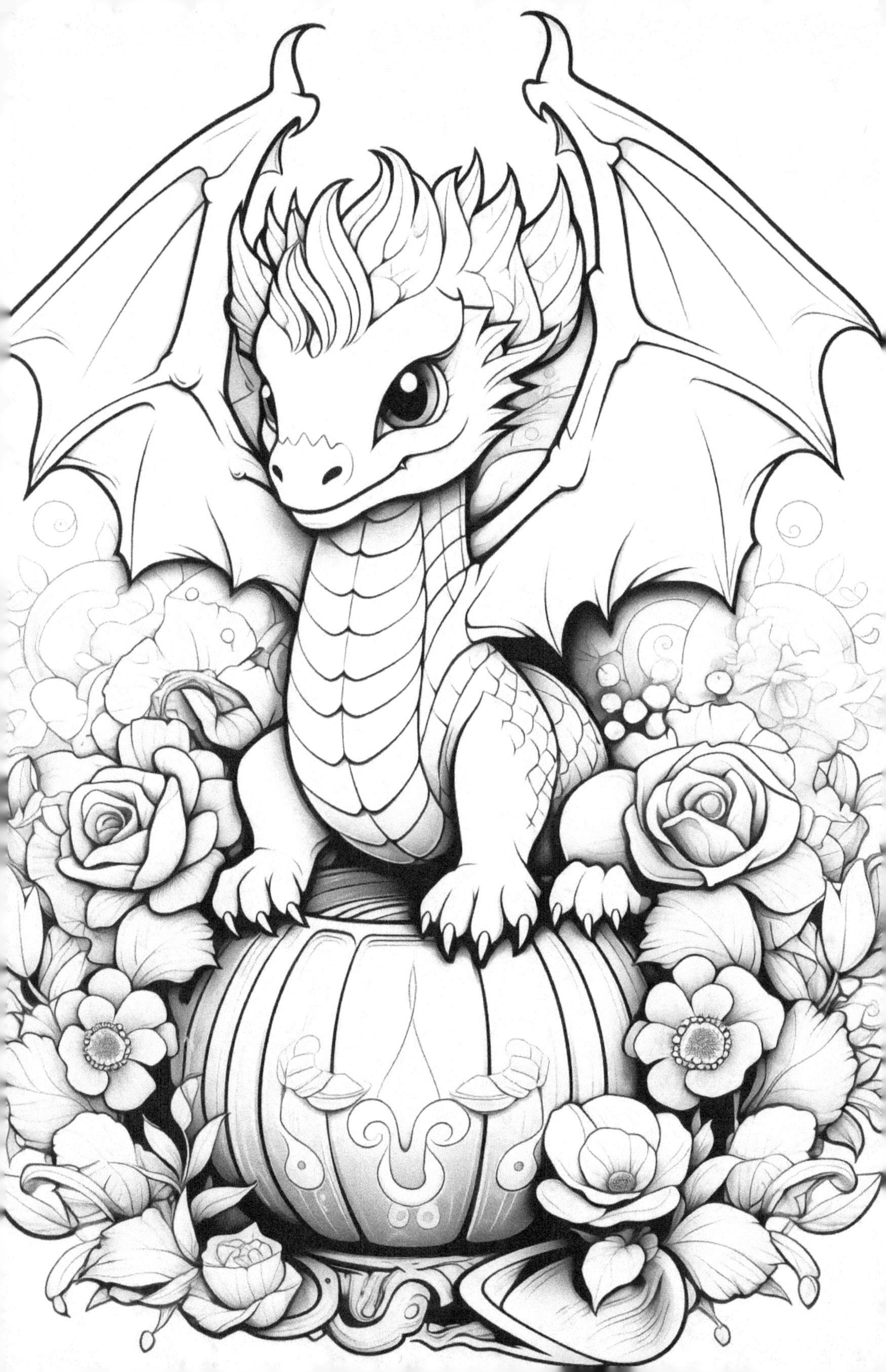

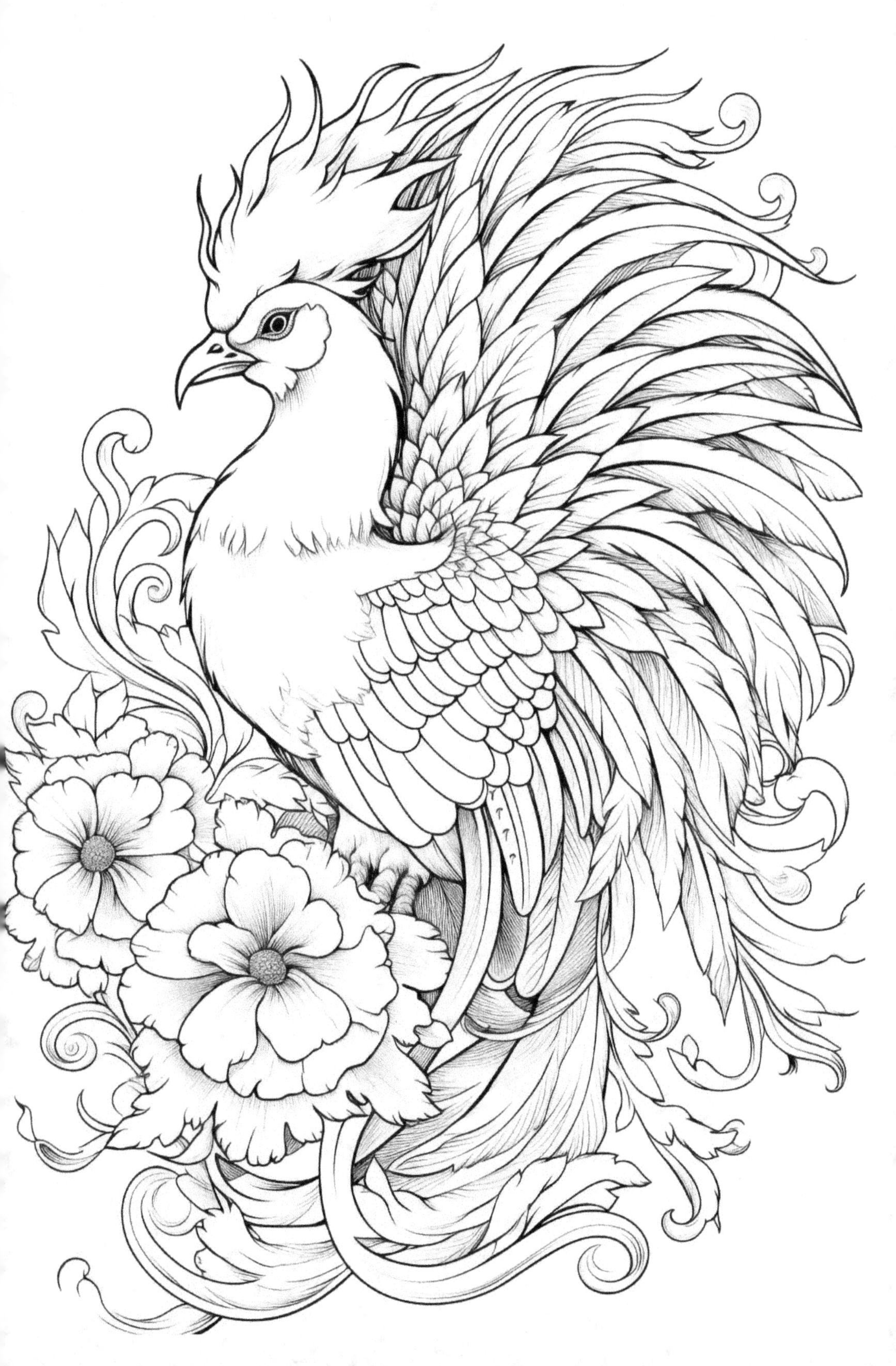

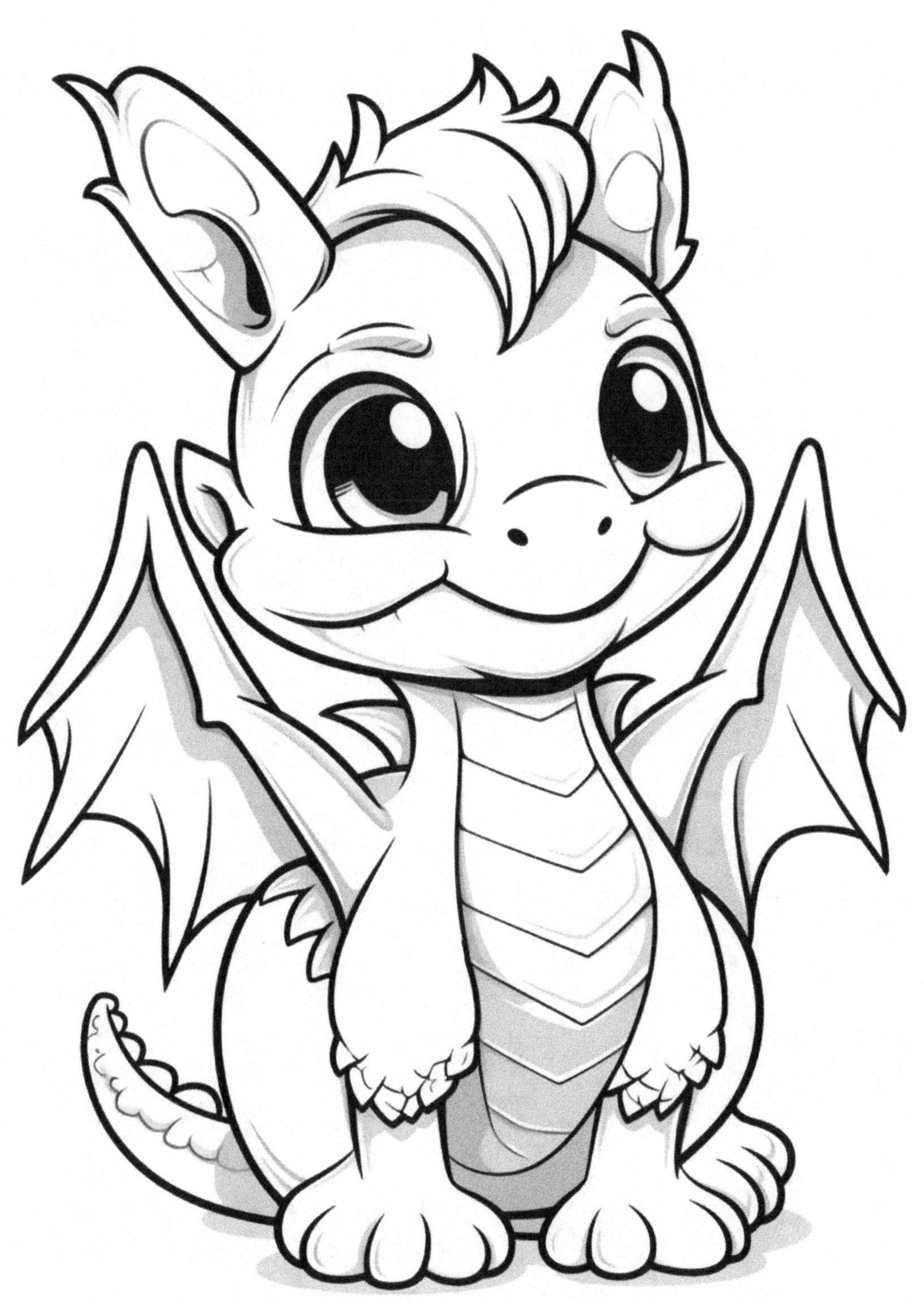

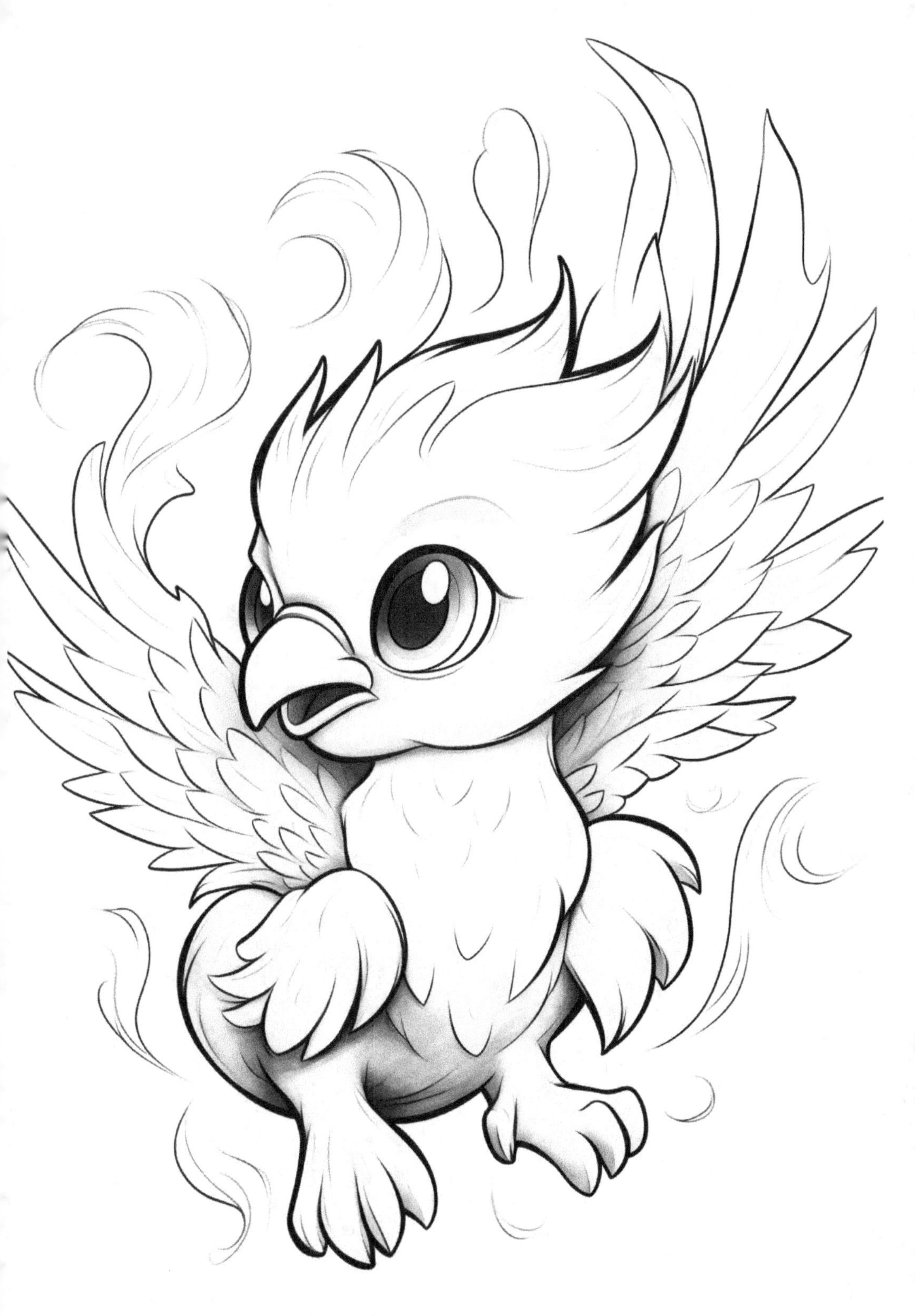

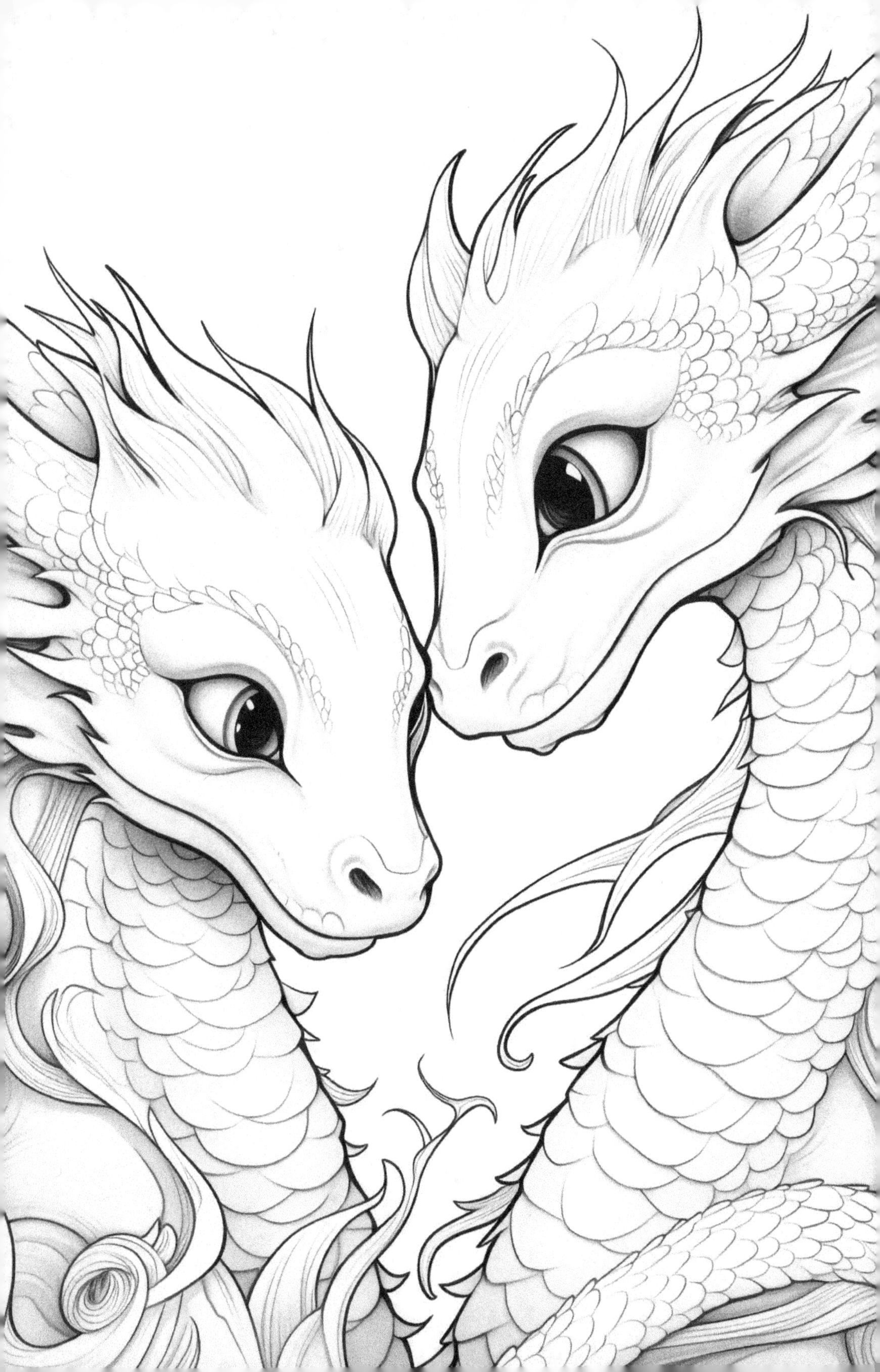

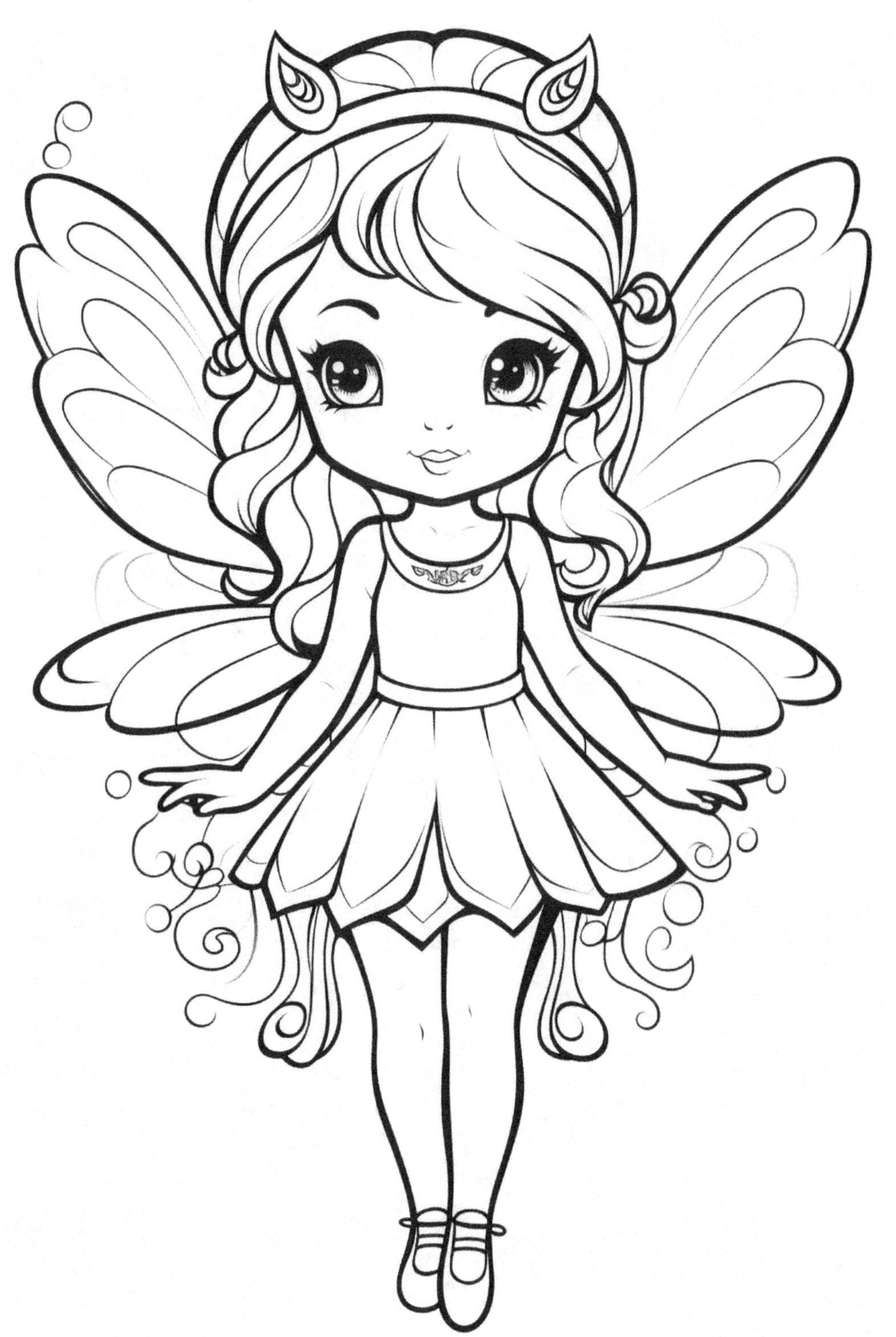

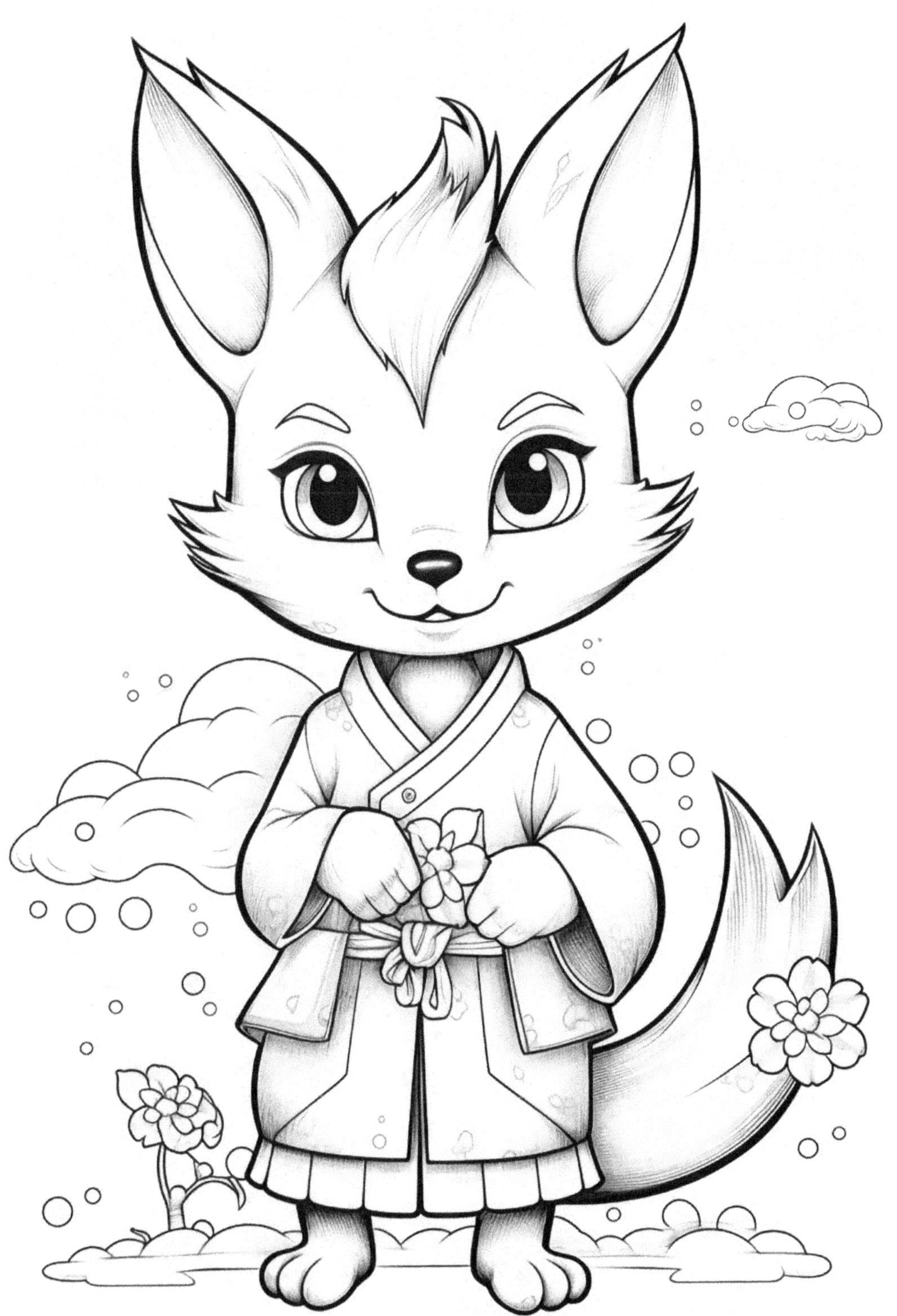

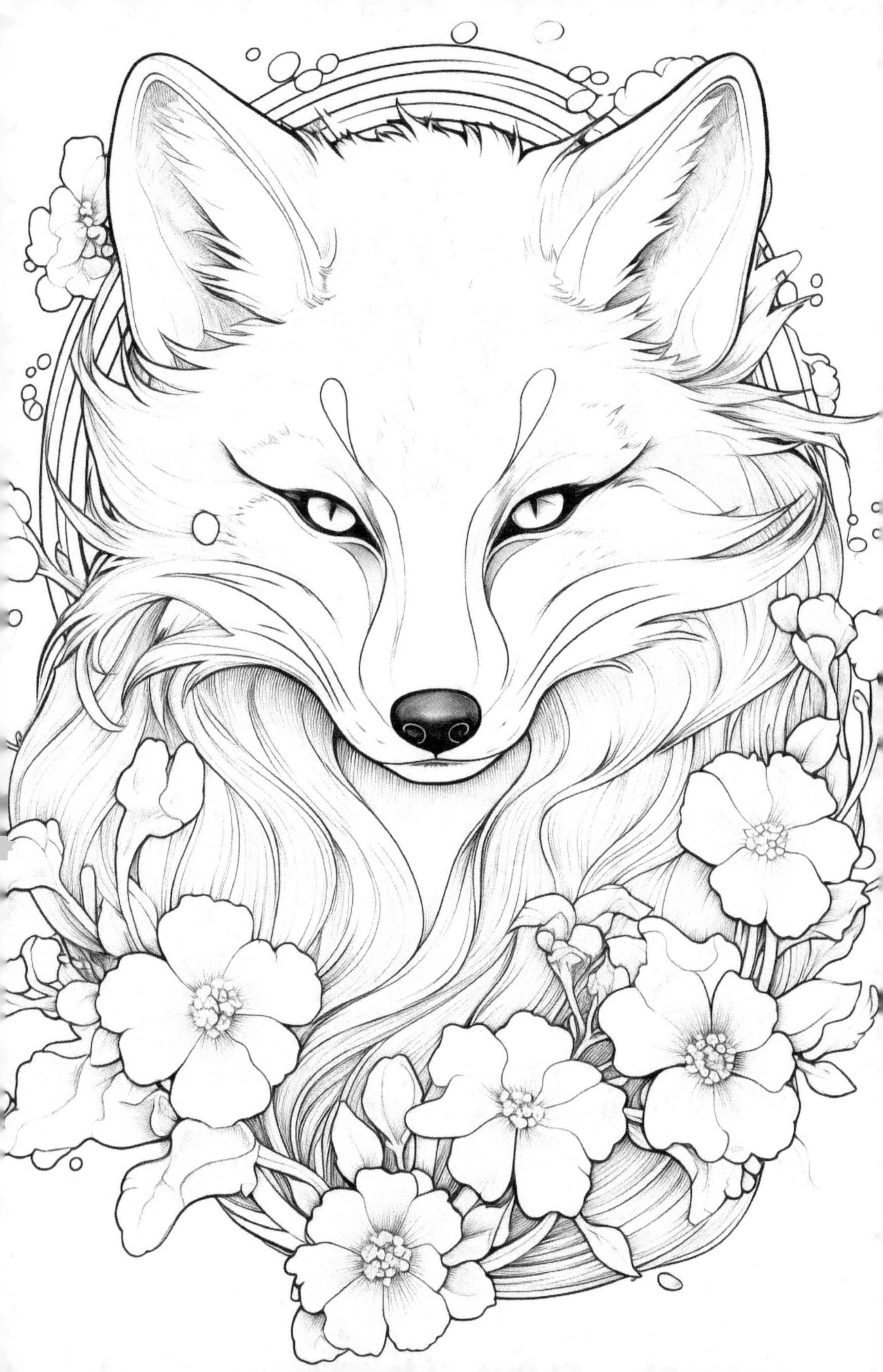

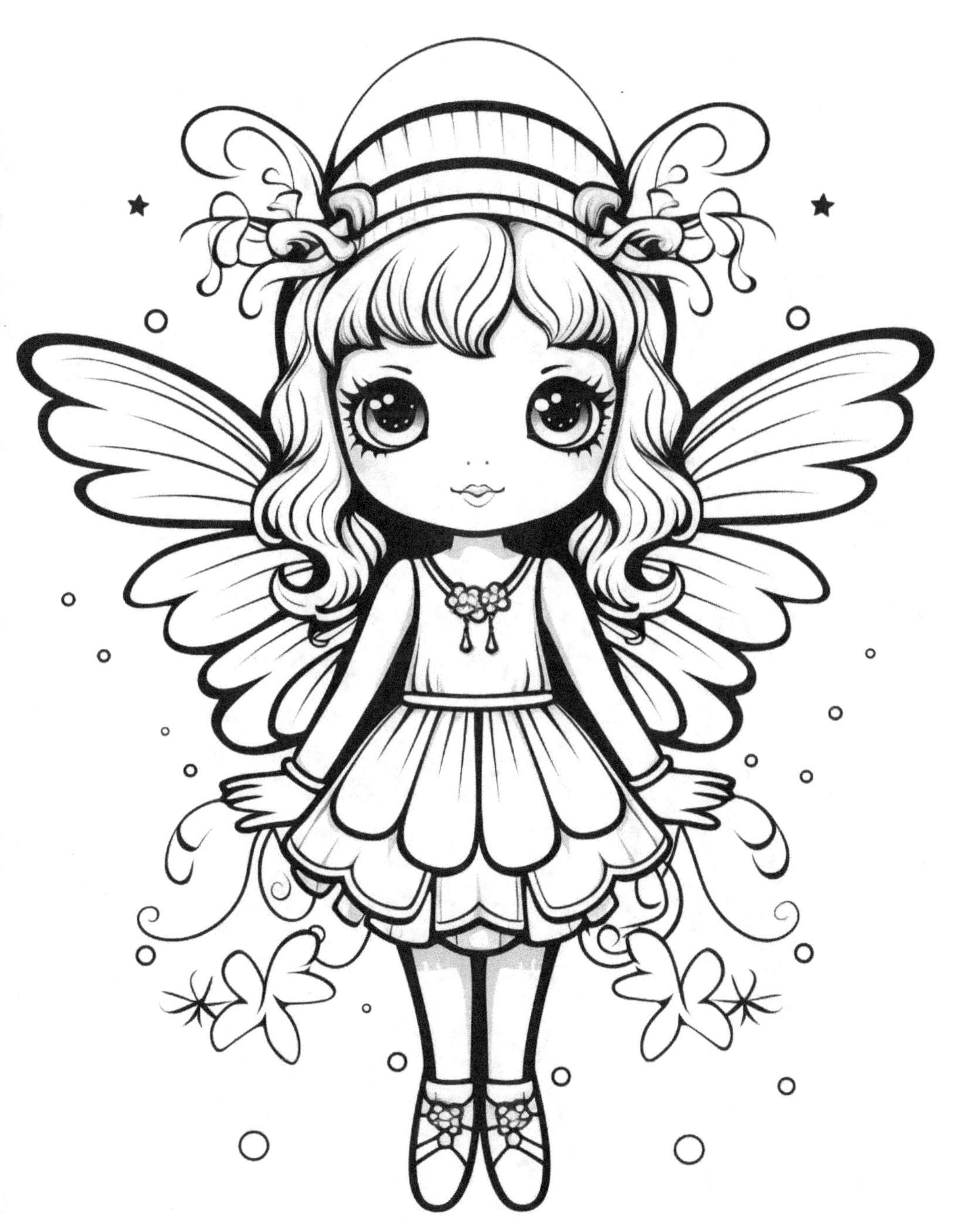

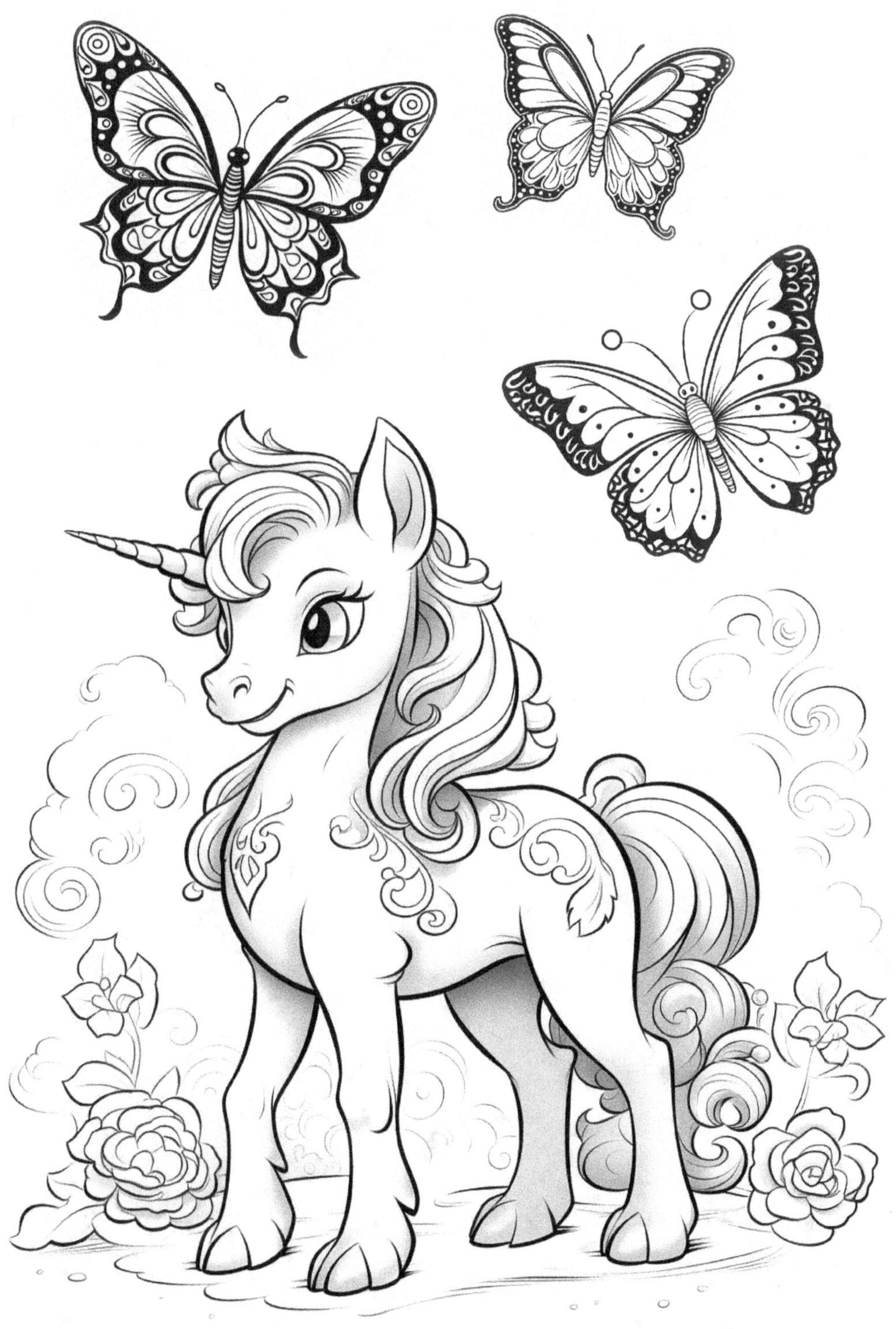

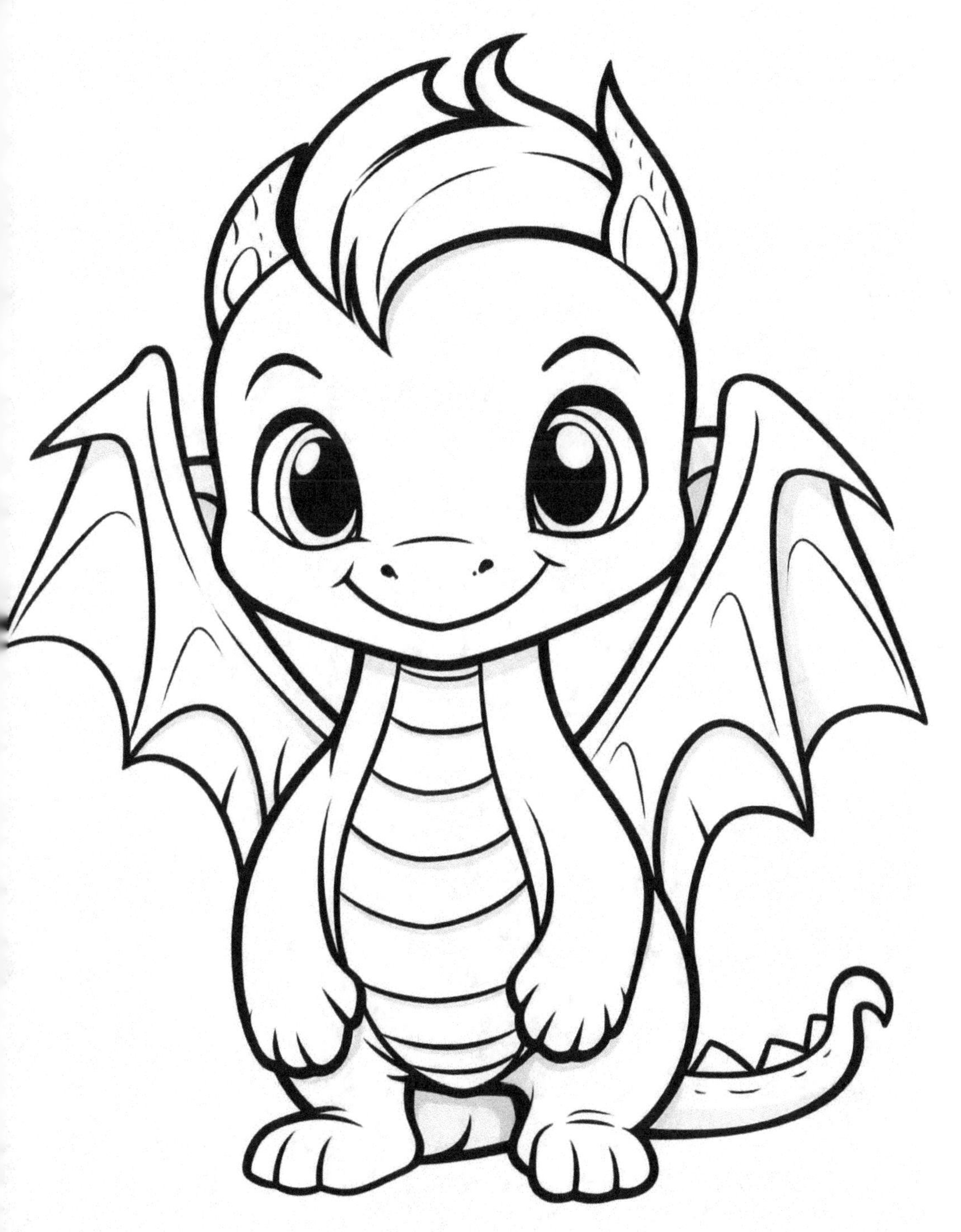

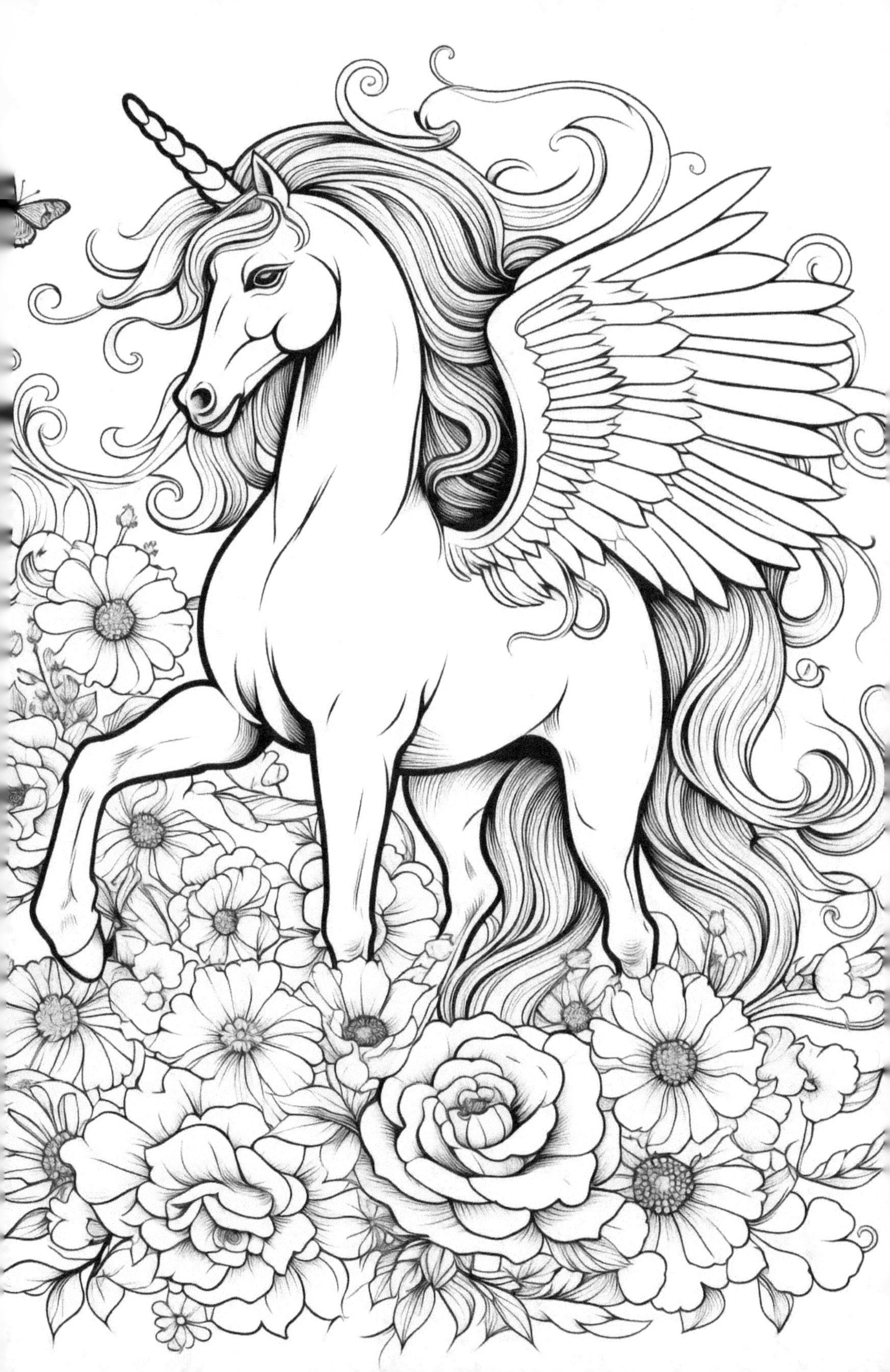

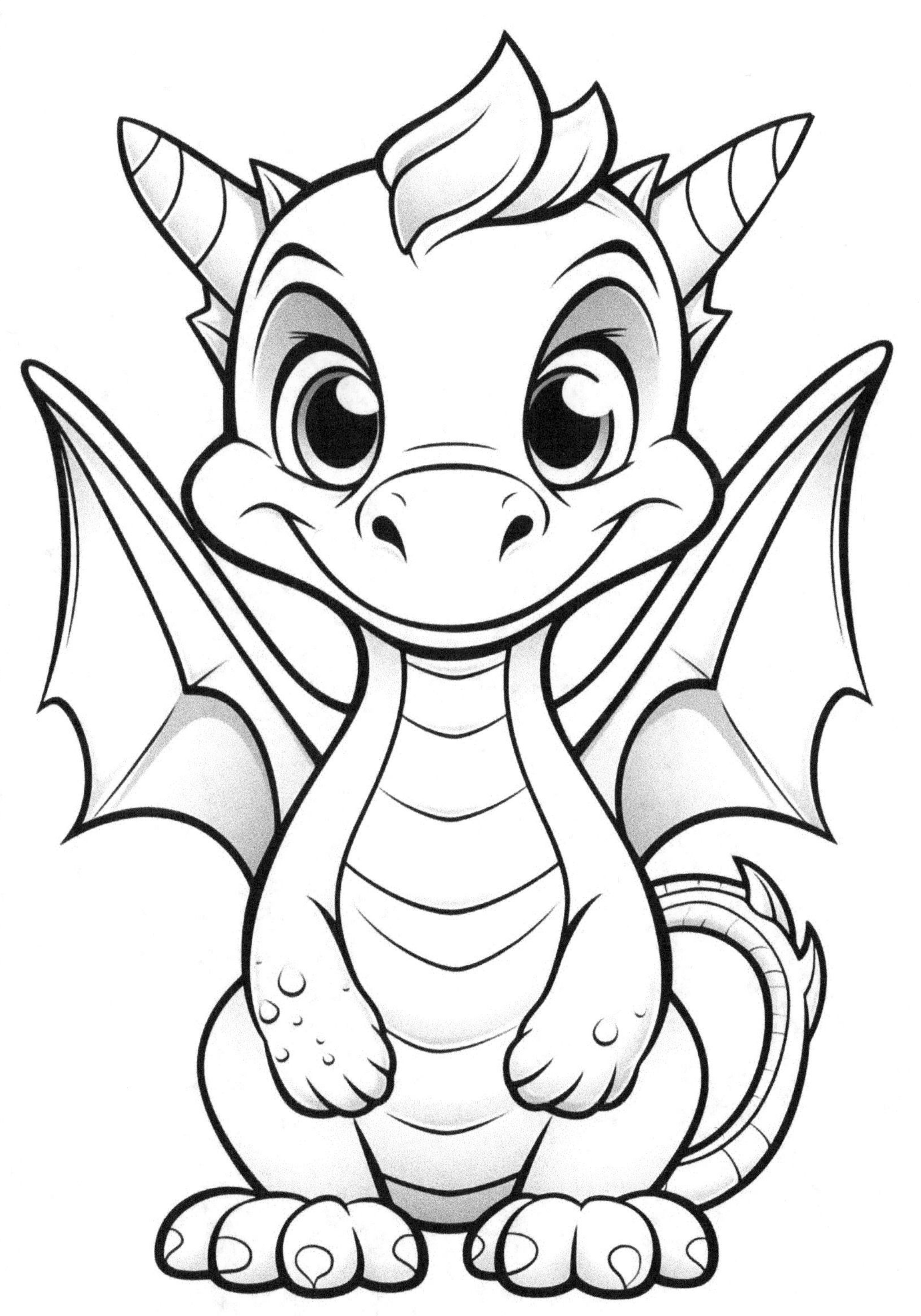

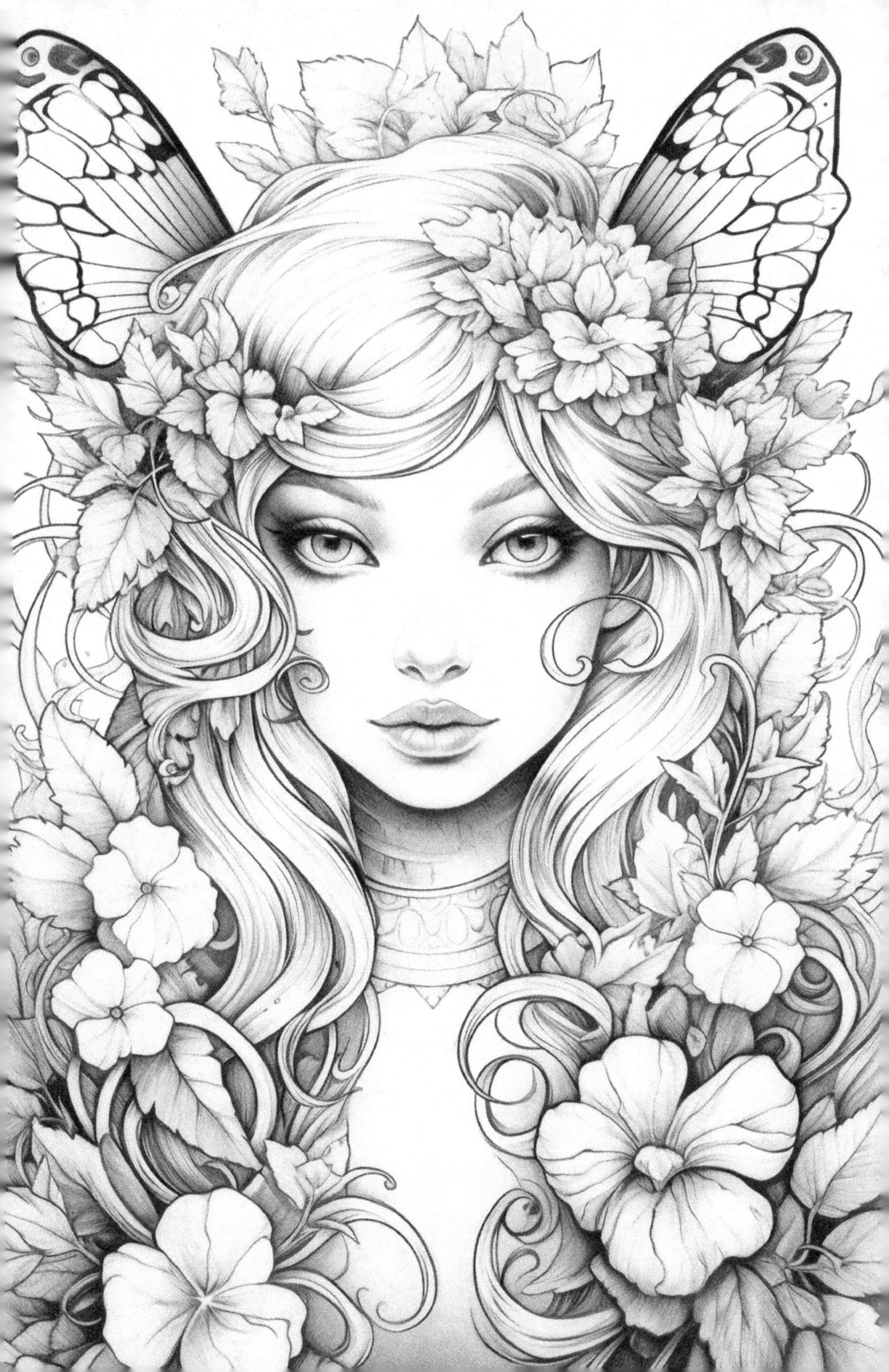

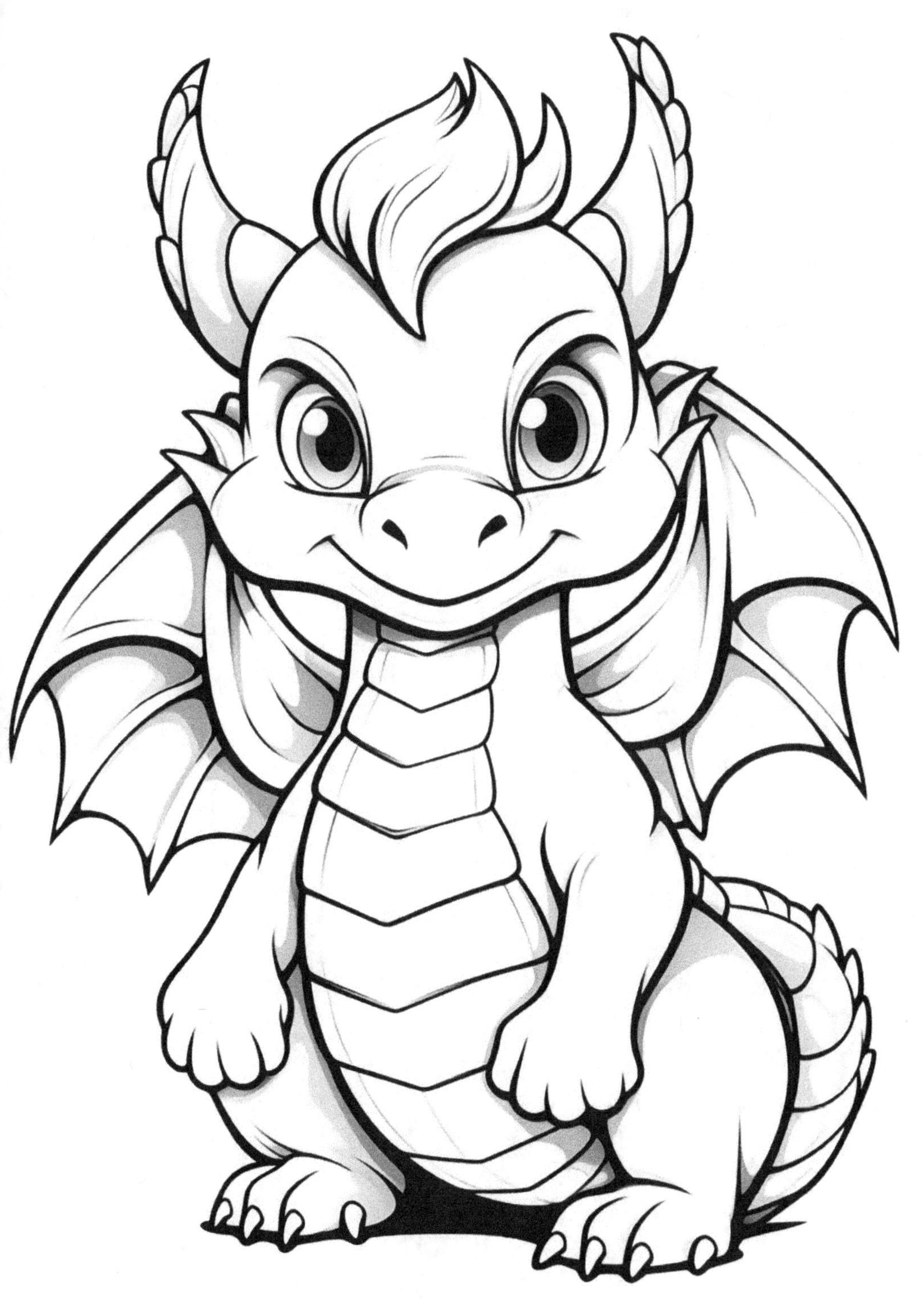

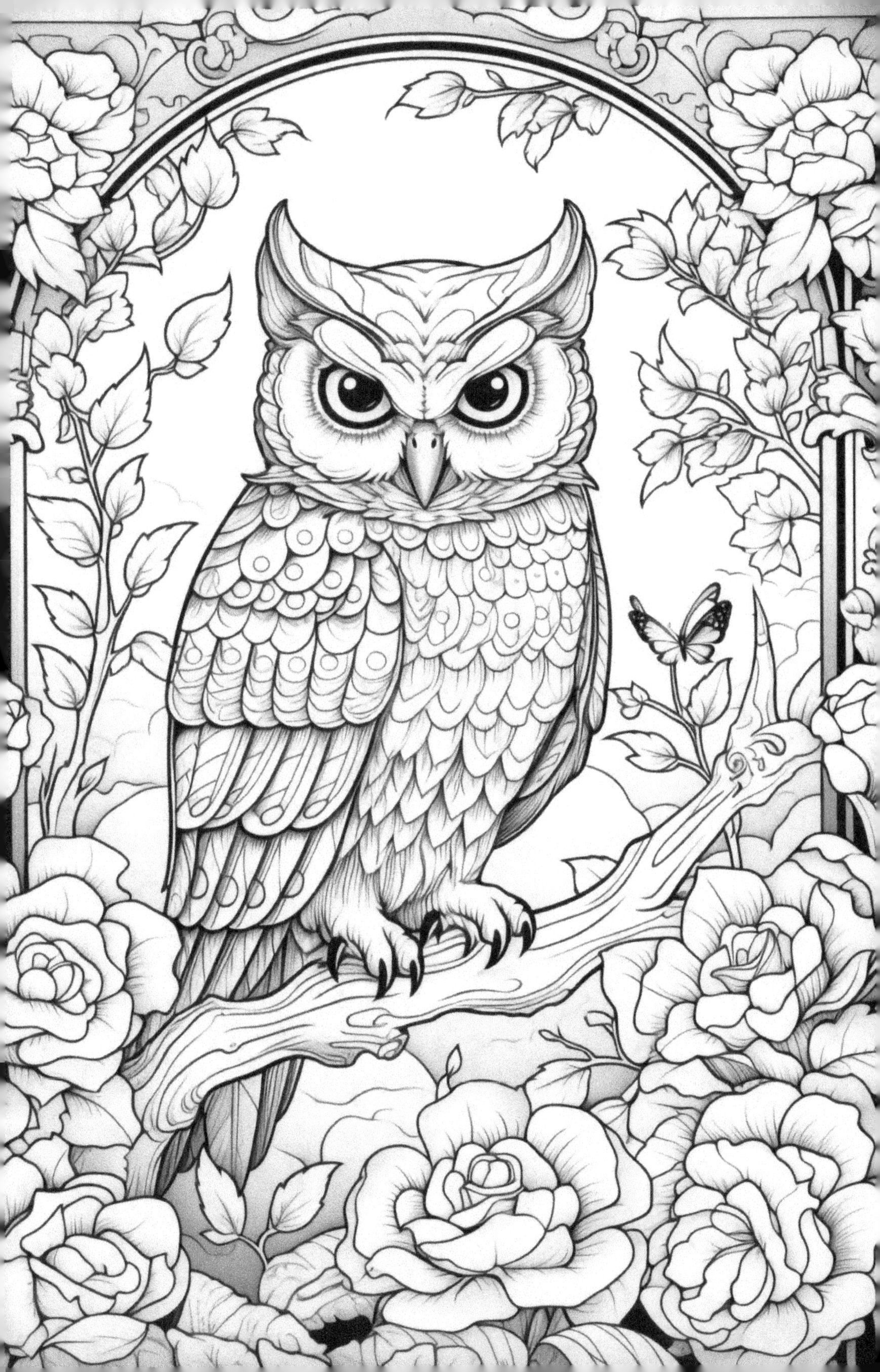

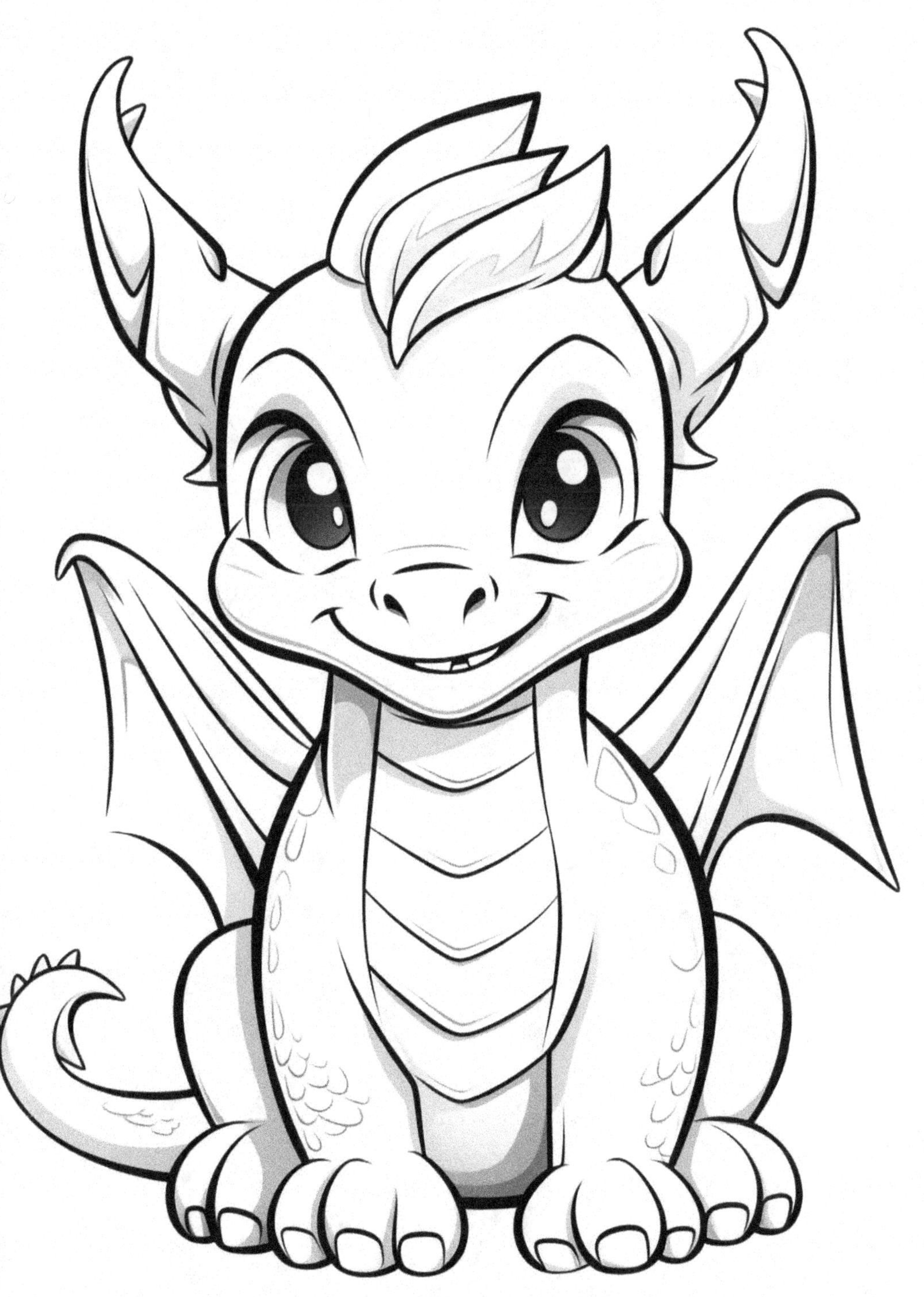

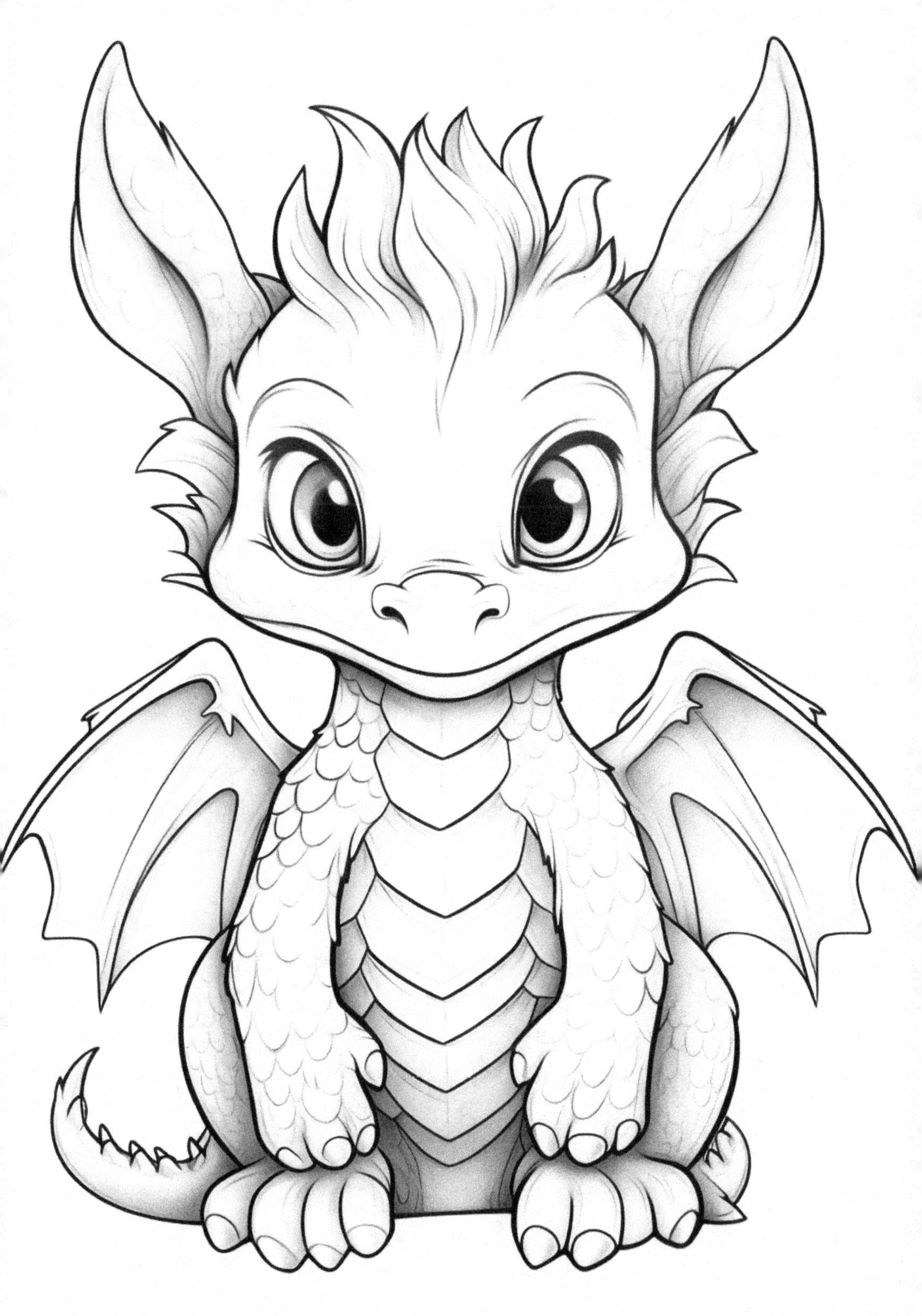

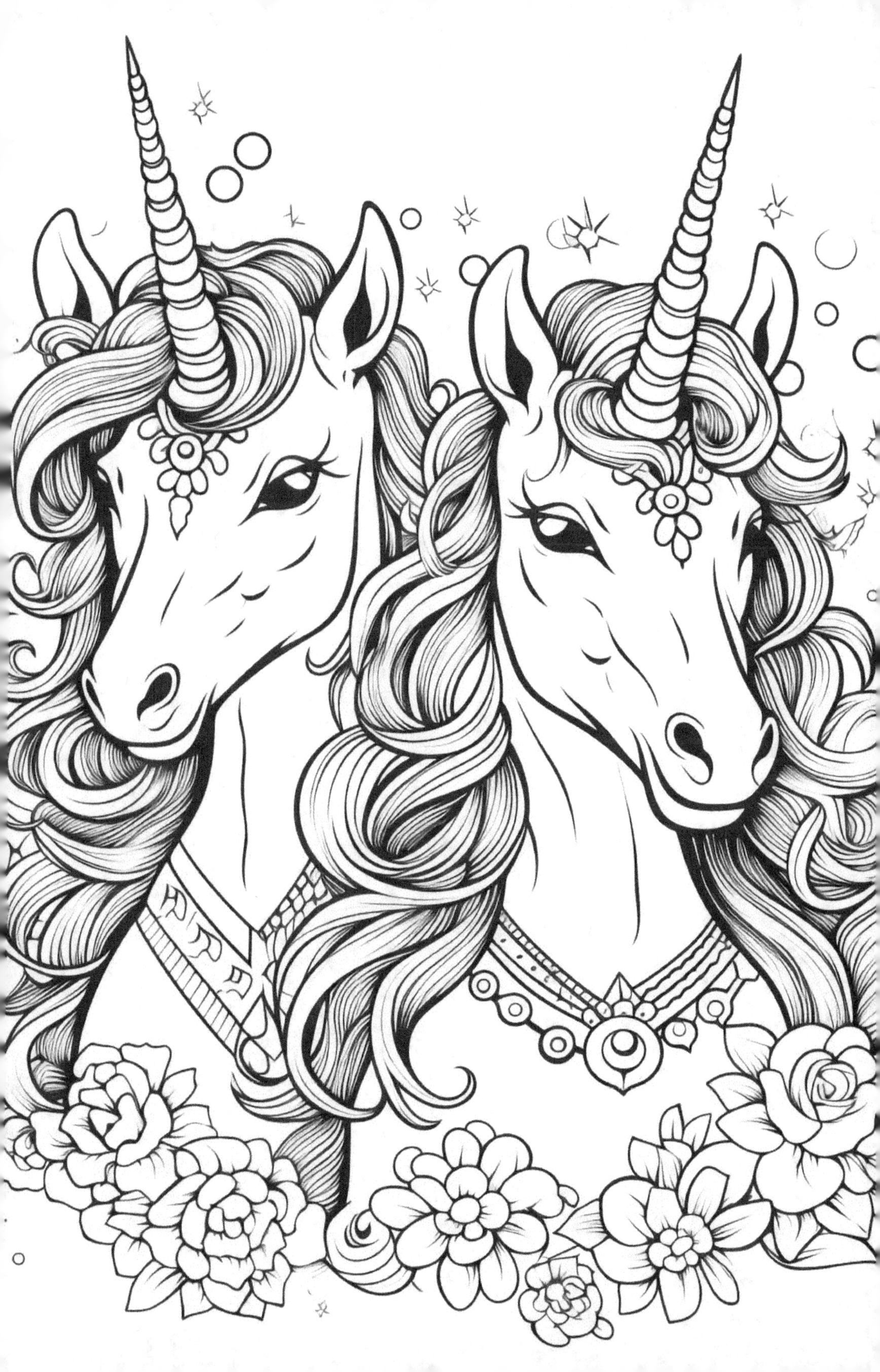

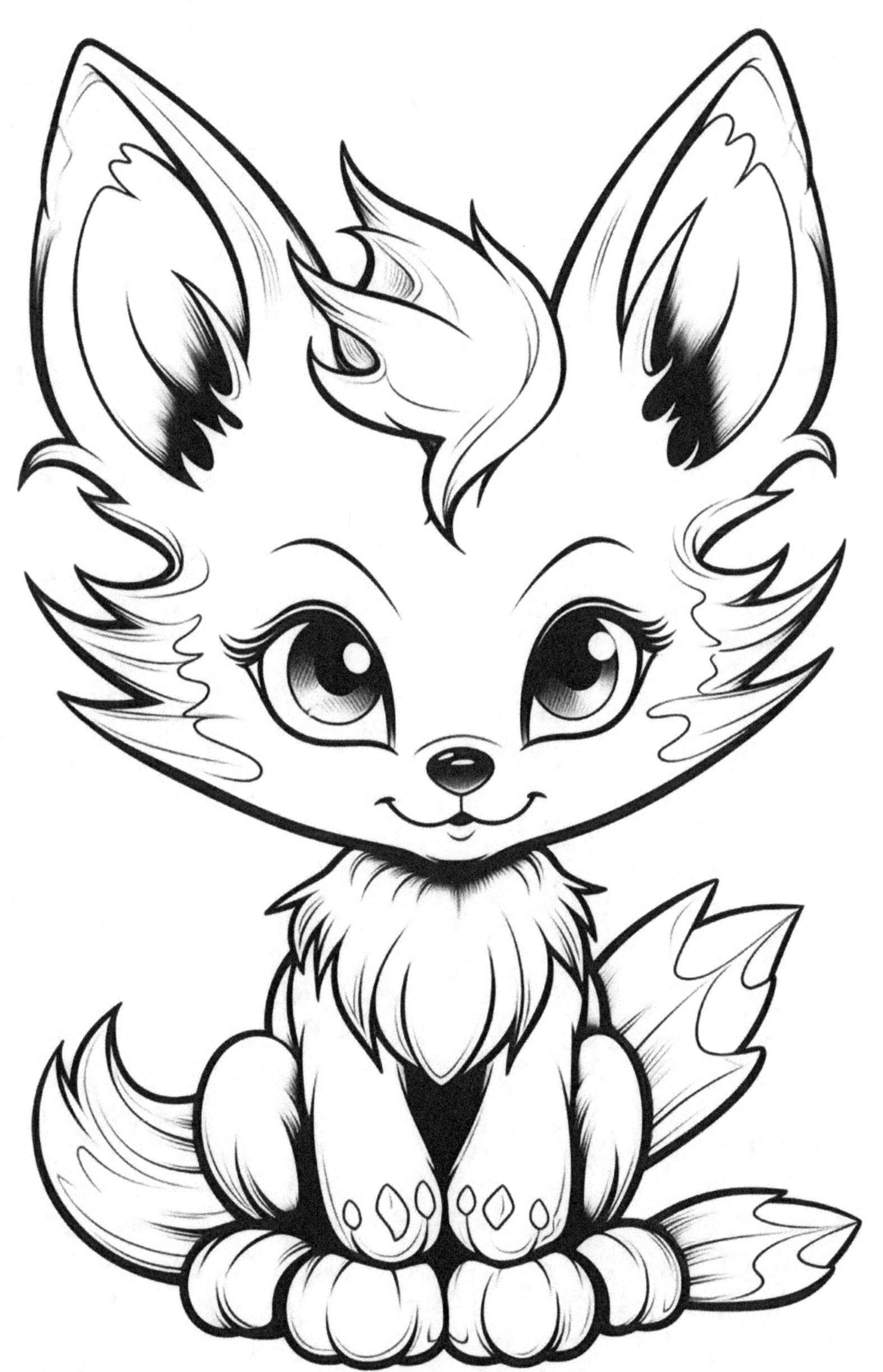

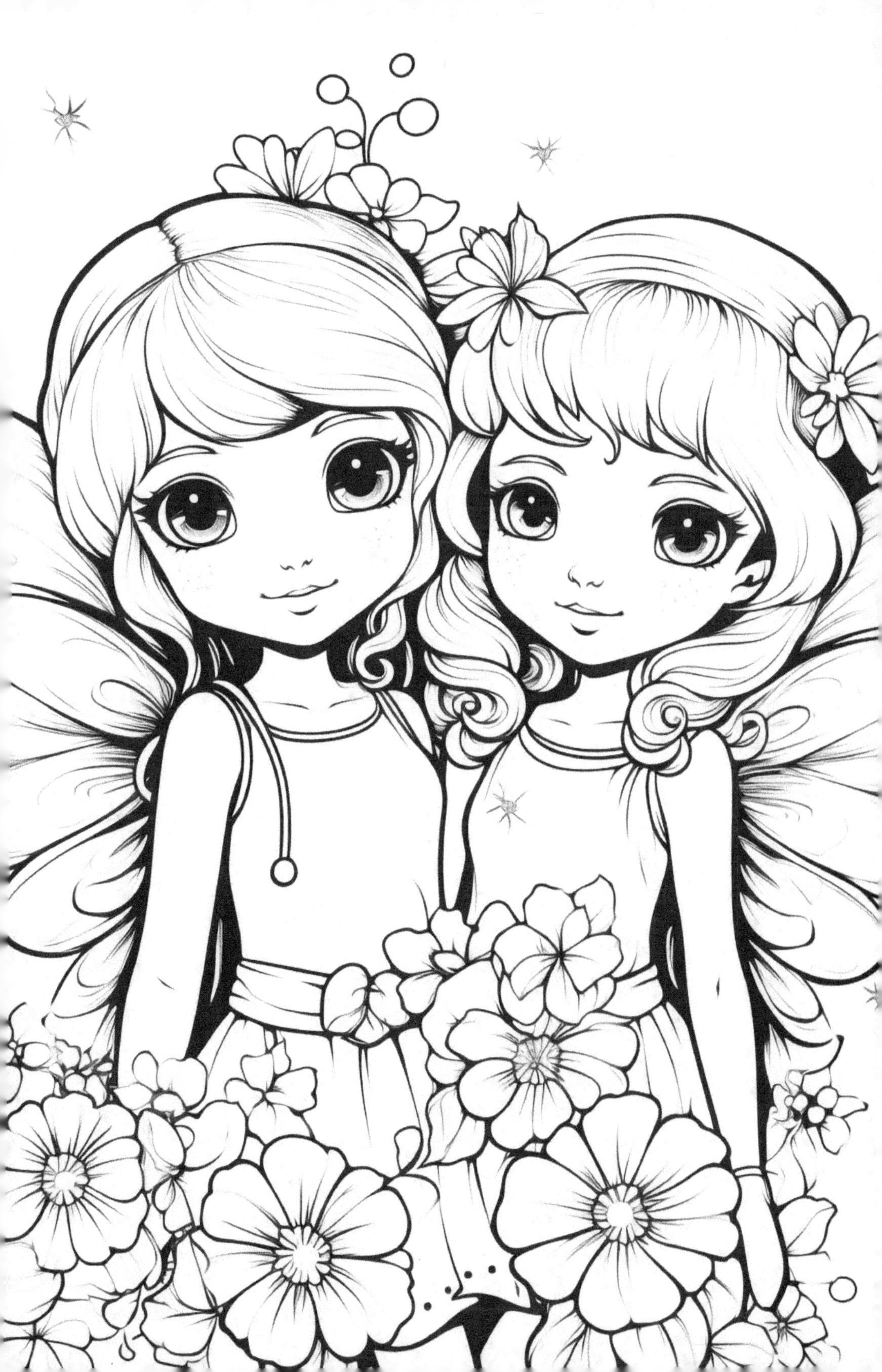

The end

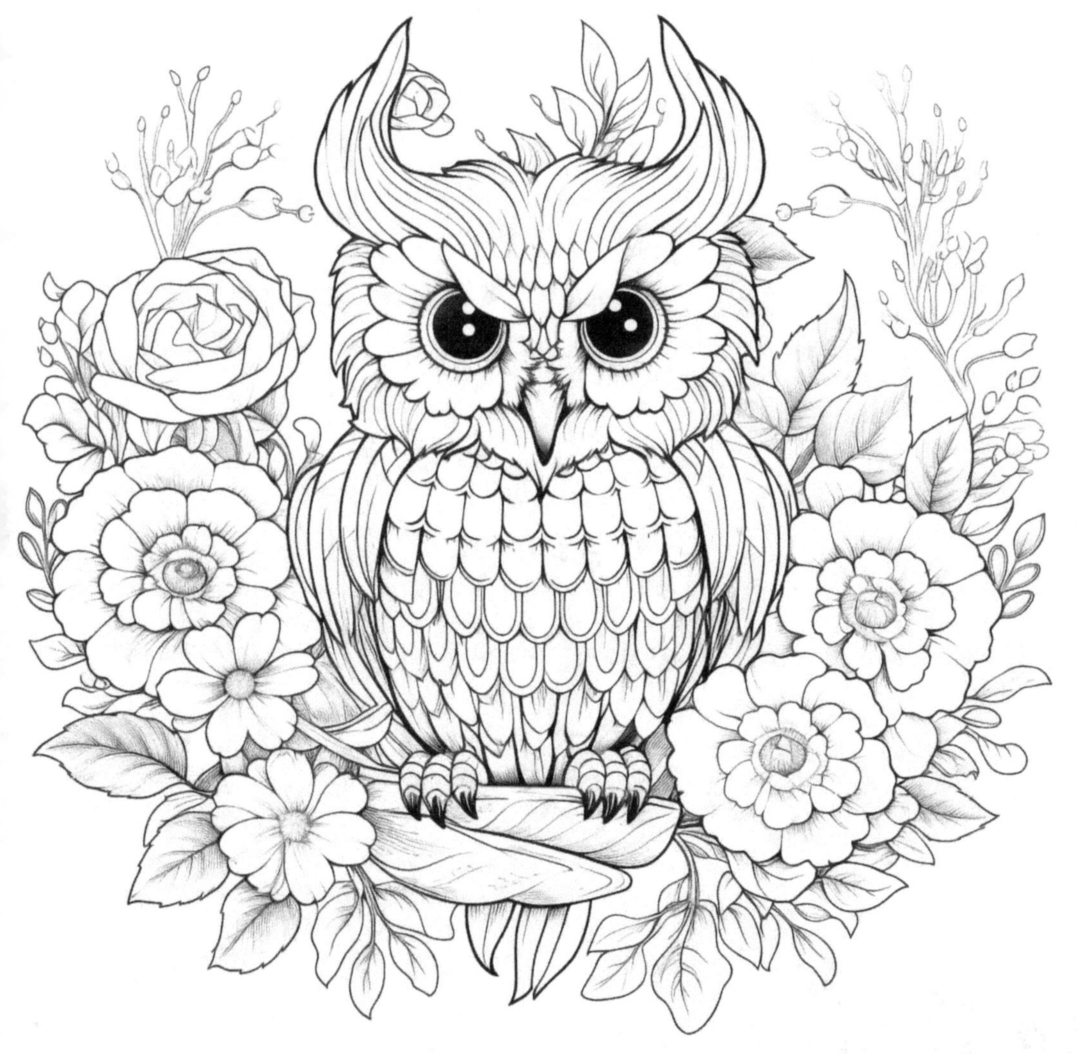

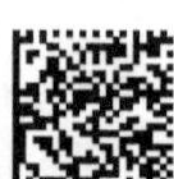

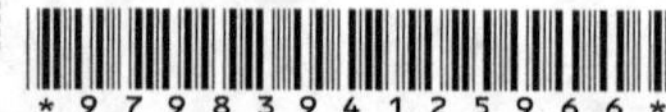